1 MONTH OF
FREE
READING

at

www.ForgottenBooks.com

By purchasing this book you are eligible for one month membership to ForgottenBooks.com, giving you unlimited access to our entire collection of over 1,000,000 titles via our web site and mobile apps.

To claim your free month visit:

www.forgottenbooks.com/free185646

ISBN 978-0-484-39927-2
PIBN 10185646

This book is a reproduction of an important historical work. Forgotten Books uses state-of-the-art technology to digitally reconstruct the work, preserving the original format whilst repairing imperfections present in the aged copy. In rare cases, an imperfection in the original, such as a blemish or missing page, may be replicated in our edition. We do, however, repair the vast majority of imperfections successfully; any imperfections that remain are intentionally left to preserve the state of such historical works.

FREEDOM OF SPEECH

AND THE ESPIONAGE ACT

Address before the New Jersey State Bar
Association at Atlantic City, N. J.,
June 18, 1921

BY

HENRY W. TAFT

OF THE NEW YORK CITY BAR

PLAINFIELD, N. J.
NEW JERSEY LAW JOURNAL PUBLISHING CO.
1921

FREEDOM OF SPEECH

AND THE ESPIONAGE ACT

Address before the New Jersey State Bar
Association at Atlantic City, N. J.,
June 18, 1921

BY

HENRY W. TAFT

OF THE NEW YORK CITY BAR

· PLAINFIELD, N. J.
NEW JERSEY LAW JOURNAL PUBLISHING CO.
1921

Reprinted from the
New Jersey Law Journal
August, 1921

FREEDOM OF SPEECH

AND THE ESPIONAGE ACT

Address before the New Jersey State Bar
Association at Atlantic City, N. J.,
June 18, 1921

BY

HENRY W. TAFT

OF THE NEW YORK CITY BAR

PLAINFIELD, N. J.
NEW JERSEY LAW JOURNAL PUBLISHING CO.
1921

Reprinted from the
New Jersey Law Journal
August, 1921

FREEDOM OF SPEECH AND
THE ESPIONAGE ACT

AMONG THE RIGHTS connoted by the term Anglo-Saxon Civil Liberty none is more vital to our institutions than that which prohibits our national legislature from making any law "abridging the freedom of speech, or of the press." This clause was not at first contained in the Constitution because the framers, and particularly Hamilton, thought it related to a matter regulated by common law and that the power to deal with it had not been delegated. But the demand of the State Conventions could not be resisted, and the provision became a part of the first of the ten Amendments.

Many of the prohibitions of these Amendments, usually referred to as the Bill of Rights, have never been resorted to. They have stood as mute, if glorious, testimony of guaranties extorted by our race from its rulers during centuries of contest and struggle; and they have served as a potential agency warning against encroachment by the State upon the rights of the individual. Thus, seldom has any attempt by any department of our national government been made to place a limit upon the freedom of oral or written expression. The first attempt, at a time of supposed national stress, led to the passage of the Sedition Law of 1798, which, with the Alien Law, met such a storm of opposition as to lead to the disastrous defeat, indeed to the disintegration of the Federalist party. The agitation against these laws undoubtedly involved a warning against any invasion of the right of free speech. But scrutiny of the proceedings of the State Legislatures of the several States, notably the extraordinary debate in the House of Delegates of Virginia; the able and exhaustive report to the House of Delegates of Virginia written by Mr. Madison, in reply to resolutions passed by the Legislatures of other States; the Kentucky resolutions of 1798 prepared by Mr. Jefferson, and other contemporary evidence, must convince the candid student of history that the defeat and destruction of the Federalist party were due, not so much to the contention that a violation of the First Amendment was threatened, as to the view, then regarded as of far greater importance, that the States had not delegated to the Federal Government the power to legislate upon the subject at all. It was the first great political battle involving the question of implied powers.

Since 1798, and until the passage of the Espionage Act of 1917, there has been no Federal statute dealing anew with the general subject of seditious utterances, and there have been in that period few if any decisions by the Supreme Court of vital importance in cases in which the protection of the First Amendment has been invoked. And yet we have passed through the great crises caused by the War of 1812, the Mexican War, which evoked much just criticism of the government, the Civil War, in which it finally became necessary to resort to the draft and there was much vocal "copperhead" sentiment, and the Spanish War. There have been virulent and unfounded attacks made upon the personal and political character of such great Presidents as Washington and Lincoln, and, in the heat of our frequently recurring Presidential elections, administrations have been subjected to criticism, sometimes verging closely upon seditious libel. But at no time has a great constitutional struggle upon the subject of free speech, like that caused in England by the *Wilkes* case, agitated the American people.

This is a remarkable evidence either of the efficacy of the First Amendment as a warning against undue aggression, or of the fact that the traditions of our race and the rules of common law were such that constitutional protection was not necessary.

But it is now asserted that the Espionage Act of 1917, as interpreted by the Supreme Court, has permitted encroachments upon the right of free speech, which are a menace to our liberties. This discouraging conclusion is maintained by a school of writers who build upon views expressed in dissenting opinions by Justices Holmes and Brandeis. Periodicals and publicists of so-called liberal tendencies have sought to arouse public interest upon the subject. But, fortunately, practical statesmen of the day do not seem to be apprehensive. When the same subject was under discussion in 1798 it attracted the attention and enlisted the services of great statesmen like Hamilton, Jefferson and Madison, and that remarkable group of lawyers and legislators who then sat in the Virginia House of Delegates, the Legislatures of Pennsylvania, New York, Massachusetts and other States, and the Federal Congress; and, naturally, the debate was on a lofty plane. To-day, however, no such intense public sentiment has been aroused. But the discussion has assumed the aspect of a manifestation of impatience with our Courts which reminds one of the recall of judges and decisions. The advocacy of such views by a minority of intellectuals is sometimes potential in producing discontent. It may do harm unless considered and fairly discussed, particularly by responsible bodies of lawyers.

The rights embodied in the great charters of our liberties have originally been asserted in connection with an actual incident in civil administration or legal procedure. That was so, for instance, in the case of the great writ of *habeas corpus*. Magna Charta and the Bill of Rights did not spring into being full-panoplied and without antecedent history. On the contrary they were the result of struggles, at long intervals and under varying circumstances, with the executive and legislative power of the State. Their guaranties always related to actual and concrete cases, and they were frequently occasioned by very homely and intrinsically unimportant episodes. When a right was secured, however, there resulted not alone a high sounding phrase, calculated to inspire lofty and patriotic sentiment, but the right asserted and the remedy guaranteed

4

acquired a vitality based on actual and frequently painful experience. There was thus forthwith embodied a concept which needed no schoolman to explain to the people. Justice Holmes has very aptly said that "the provisions of the Constitution are not mathematical formulas having their essence in their form; they are organic living institutions transplanted from English soil. Their significance is vital, not formal; it is to be gathered not simply by taking the words and a dictionary, but by considering their origin and the line of their growth." (Gompers v. U. S., 233 U. S. 604, 610).

Our Constitution was conceived in this practical spirit. It must be applied in the same spirit. The question whether it has been violated must be settled by visualizing a real controversy, tried out according to time-honored methods of procedure. If we idealize such a right as the freedom of speech and apply an academic test to the verdict of a jury or a charge of a Court we may easily find material for discontent, and it will be but one step further for an enthusiast or a theorist to conclude that the palladium of our liberties is imperilled. Thus in the *Abrams, Schaeffer* and *Pierce* cases, where the Supreme Court refused to set aside verdicts of guilty for violations of the Espionage Act, a Harvard Professor of Law charged the Supreme Court with being "careless in its safeguarding of the fundamental human need of freedom of speech" and reached the despairing conclusion that the decisions reduced the "great principle behind" the First Amendment "almost to a pious hope." This attitude of mind has led this same author to make an extended adverse criticism of the decision of the Court in the *Abrams* case, in a chapter[2] filled with extraneous matter which would be inadmissible in any actual trial. But decisions upon violations of the Espionage Act must have applied to them the tests not different from those in cases having less historical significance. In the case of *Schaeffer*,[3] indicted for a violation of the Espionage Act, Justice Brandeis (Justice Holmes concurring) said that the decision of the majority of the Court subjected "to new perils the constitutional liberty of the press, already seriously curtailed in practice under powers assumed to have been conferred upon the postal authorities. Nor will this grave danger end with the passing of the War." But Justice Clark, while he joined in the dissent, expressed what seems to me the more correct view, that the decision did not involve "a great peril either to the maintenance of law and order and governmental authority on the one hand, or to the freedom of the press on the other."

The extreme contention of the present day critics of the Espionage Act is that, since the common law doctrine of seditious libel, which condemns all writings tending to bring into contempt the Church, the State, the officers of government, or the administration of the law, has been prohibited by the First Amendment, it must likewise follow that a person cannot be condemned for the "bad intent" of a statement or a writing, except where there is an actual incitement to crime with a prospect of being successful.

This theory, it will be admitted, would go far toward depriving the

---

[2]Chapter III, entitled "A Contemporary State Trial" in "Freedom of Speech," by Zechariah Chafee, Jr., Professor of Law in Harvard University.
[3]251 U. S. 466.

government of the power of self-protection in times of stress. If prosecution for seditious libel were resorted to, as it has been in other countries, to sustain a dynasty or to prevent an impairment of the sanctity of the divine right of kings, we will all agree that anything resembling a power to cause such a repression would be contrary to the spirit of our institutions. Nor will it be seriously contended that criticism or abuse of even the President of the United States, falling short of what would justify a suit for libel, could be penalized by Act of Congress. But that the "bad intent" of a writing is to be inferred only from its contents, its tendency to produce disorder or crime, or the violent overthrow of our government, and from the clear and present danger that it will be successful, is the proposition that seems now to be maintained by some of those who are criticizing the recent decisions of the Supreme Court on the Espionage Act.[4]

The case of *Schenck* v. *The United States*[5] was decided in 1918 by a unanimous Court, Justice Holmes writing the opinion. The prosecution was on an indictment for circulating a document, the clear purpose of which was to incite to a violation of the Conscription Act. But it was claimed that what was said was in important parts what had been said by well known public men, and the Court admitted that in "many places and in ordinary times the defendants in saying all that was said in the circular would have been within their constitutional rights. *But the character of every act depends upon the circumstances in which it is done. The most stringent protection of free speech would not protect a man in falsely shouting fire in a theatre and causing a panic. It does not even protect a man from an injunction against uttering words that may have all the effect of force. . . .* The question in every case is whether the words used are used in such circumstances and are of such a nature as to create a clear and present danger that they will bring about the substantive evils that Congress has a right to prevent. *It is a question of proximity and degree.* When a nation is at war many things that might be said in time of peace will not be endured so long as men fight and no Court could regard them as protected by any constitutional right."

Justice Holmes adds, and these words are to be remembered in connection with his subsequent dissent in the *Abrams* and other Espionage cases:

"The statute of 1917 in Sec. 4 punishes conspiracies to obstruct as well as actual obstruction. If the act, (speaking, or circulating a paper), its tendency and the intent with which it is done are the same, *we perceive no ground for saying that success alone warrants making the act a crime.*"

The *Schenck* case was followed by the *Frohwerk* case,[6] where there was an indictment for conspiracy to violate the Espionage Act in inducing by newspaper publications a refusal to do military duty. Justice Holmes, writing the opinion, said that the First Amendment "cannot have been, and obviously was not, intended to give immunity for every possible use of language." He added:

---

[4] The discussion is confined chiefly to the decisions under Sections 3 and 4 of Title I. I do not deal with Censorship, or Exclusion from the Mails, or with Interstate Commerce.

[5] 249 U. S. 47, 50.

[6] 249 U. S. 204, 205.

6

"We venture to believe that neither Hamilton nor Madison nor any other competent person, then or later, ever supposed that to make criminal the counselling of a murder within the jurisdiction of Congress would be an unconstitutional interference with free speech."

The *Debs* case[7] was a prosecution for an obstruction of the recruiting and enlistment service. Justice Holmes, writing the opinion of a unanimous court, approved, at least by implication, a charge to the jury that they could not find against the defendant "unless the words used had as their *natural tendency* and *reasonably probable* effect to obstruct the recruiting service, etc., and unless the defendant had the specific intent to do so in his mind." It will be observed that this charge does not require that the words shall be such "as to create a *clear and present* danger" that they *will bring about the substantive evils aimed at*. And if that were the requirement of the law in all cases, it would involve a degree of certitude and proximity which would probably rarely occur, and which would be a test coming quite close to "saying that success alone warrants making the act a crime," which the Court in the *Schenck* case said went too far. But the nature of the case does not require a rule of causation more stringent than is usual in criminal trials. To require, as in the *Debs* case, that an effect shall have a "natural tendency" and a "reasonably probable effect," satisfies every requirement, and it is fair to assume that the Court intended by the phraseology used in that case to indicate, not a modification of the rule expressed in the *Schenck* case, but an interpretation of its unnecessarily emphatic and comprehensive language.

I have devoted some attention to this subject because in the dissenting opinions of Justices Holmes and Brandeis, in some of the later cases, they seem to have assumed that the words "clear and present danger" were to be accepted as an unvarying formula for the guidance of Judges and juries.

I now reach a consideration of the notable case of *Abrams* v. *United States*,[8] which has caused heated controversy. Justice Clark wrote the opinion of the Court, and Justice Brandeis a dissenting opinion in which Justice Holmes concurred. The defendants were charged with a conspiracy to violate the provisions of the Espionage Act in uttering writings which it was variously charged tended to incite resistance to the United States in time of war and the curtailment of the production of ammunition and other things necessary to the prosecution of the war. The defendants were Russian citizens and avowed themselves to be revolutionists in sympathy with the principles of the Russian revolution. The principal claim made by them and the chief ground urged in the dissenting opinion was that the primary purpose of the writings complained of was to prevent an injury to the cause of the Russian revolution by the sending of American troops into Russia to fight the Bolshevists, and that any effect of the writings of the defendants in obstructing war measures against Germany were indirect, incidental and too remote to justify an inference of criminal intent. But the question came before the Court on a question of law, viz: "Whether there was *some* evidence

---

[7]249 U. S. 211.
[8]250 U. S. 616.

competent and substantial before the jury. *fairly tending* to sustain the verdict." The consequences of this situation have sometimes been overlooked, although lawyers will recognize it as presenting a narrow field of inquiry for an appellate court; and some of the most insistent critics have seemed to assume that, on the question of bad intent and probable effect, the case was thrown open to the Court for consideration as if it had the full power to consider facts from which divergent inferences could be drawn—in other words that they could usurp the function of the jury.

To the claim that the defendants only intended to prevent injury to the Russian cause, the Court said:

"Men must be held to have intended, and to be accountable for, the effects which their acts are likely to produce. Even if their primary purpose and intent was to aid the cause of the Russian Revolution, the plan of action which they adopted necessarily involved, before it could be realized, defeat of the war program of the United States, for the obvious effect of this appeal, if it should become effective, as they hoped it might, would be to persuade persons of character, such as those whom they regarded themselves as addressing, not to aid government loans and not to work in ammunition factories, where their work would produce 'bullets, bayonets, cannon' and other munitions of war, the use of which would cause the 'murder' of Germans and Russians."

Referring to another part of the circular, which states that America has betrayed the workers and that there should be a "general strike" for an "open challenge only will let the government know that not only the Russian worker fights for freedom, but also here in America lives the spirit of revolution," the Court said that "the manifest purpose of such a publication was to create an attempt to defeat the war plans of the government of the United States, by bringing upon the country the paralysis of a general strike, thereby arresting the production of all munitions and other things essential to the conduct of the war;" and, again, that "the plain purpose of their propaganda was to excite, at the supreme crisis of the war, disaffection, sedition, riots, and, as they hoped, revolution, in this country, for the purpose of embarrassing and, if possible, defeating the military plans of the government in Europe. And the Court concluded that it was "clear not only that some evidence but that much persuasive evidence was before the jury tending to prove that the defendants were guilty."

Justice Holmes based his dissent upon the ground that the conduct of the defendant was not "with intent" to curtail production of munitions, etc., so as "to cripple or hinder the United States in the prosecution of the war," because a man "does not do the act with intent to produce it unless the aim to produce it is the proximate motive of the specific act, although there may be some deeper motive behind." And then he lays down the "clear and imminent danger" rule formulated in his opinion in the *Schenck* case.

The substance of Justice Holmes' contention was that the only object of the paper objected to was "to help Russia and stop American intervention there against the popular government—not to impede the United States in the war that it was carrying on. To say that two phrases taken literally might import a suggestion of conduct that would

8

have interference with the war as an indirect and probably undesired effect seems to me by no means enough to show an attempt to produce that effect." But in the *Debs* case, where bad intent was inferred from a speech mainly dealing with socialism, Justice Holmes had said that "if a part of the manifest intent of the more general utterances was to encourage those present to obstruct the recruiting service, and if in passages such encouragement was directly given, the immunity of the general theme may not be enough to protect the speech;" and he added that the evidence justified the conclusion that the bad intent existed.

The primary and ostensible purpose of the paper complained of in the *Abrams* case was to oppose sending troops to Russia, but the substantial effect of it was to obstruct the prosecution of the war. If the rule of primary, and not secondary or consequential, intent should be applied, as Judge Holmes urged that it should be, the ingenuity of persons disapproving the prosecution of the war and skilled in the modern art of subtle propaganda would be employed in devising means by which, while seeming to advocate by speech purposes not within the reach of the Espionage Act, would have had the efficient result of obstructing the prosecution of the war. The opinion of the majority of the Court is far more consonant with the ordinary rule applied in jury cases where questions of "proximity and degree" involving intent are under consideration. The rest of Justice Holmes's opinion deals in an admirable way with the general subject of liberty of speech.[9] It has been much quoted, particularly by those who have criticized the opinion of the majority of the Court. In my view it has very little to do with the question of intent or the procedural situation which the Court had to deal with. It seems to have been evoked

---

[9]"Persecution," said Justice Holmes, "for the expression of opinions seems to me perfectly logical. If you have no doubt of your premises or your power and want a certain result with all your heart you naturally express your wishes in law and sweep away all opposition. To allow opposition by speech seems to indicate that you think the speech impotent, as when a man says he has squared the circle, or that you do not care whole-heartedly for the result, or that you doubt either your power or your premises. But when men have realized that time has upset many fighting faiths, they may come to believe, even more than they believe the very foundations of their own conduct, that the ultimate good desired is better reached by free trade in ideas—that the best test of truth is the power of the thought to get itself accepted in the competition of the market, and that truth is the only ground upon which their wishes safely can be carried out. That at any rate is the theory of our Constitution. It is an experiment, as all life is an experiment. Every year if not every day we have to wager our salvation upon some prophecy based upon imperfect knowledge. While that experiment is part of our system I think that we should be eternally vigilant against attempts to check the expression of opinions that we loathe and believe to be fraught with death, unless they so imminently threaten immediate interference with the lawful and pressing purposes of the law that an immediate check is required to save the country. I wholly disagree with the argument of the Government that the First Amendment left the common law as to seditious libel in force. History seems to me against the notion. I had conceived that the United States through many years had shown its repentance for the Sedition Act of 1798, by repaying fines that it imposed. Only the emergency that makes it immediately dangerous to leave the correction of evil counsels to time warrants making any exception to the sweeping command, 'Congress shall make no law abridging the freedom of speech.' Of course I am speaking only of expression of opinion and exhortations, which were all that were uttered here, but I regret that I cannot put into more impressive words my belief that in their conviction upon this indictment the defendants were deprived of their rights under the Constitution of the United States."

by the revulsion of feeling caused by what the Justice regarded as an excessive sentence of twenty years imprisonment imposed on the defendant. But whatever the inspiration the result is a most eloquent statement of the principle underlying the doctrine of Freedom of Speech which may well take rank with the reasoning in "Mill on Liberty" and Milton in the "Areopagitica." It contains the following aphoristic and much quoted sentence:

"But when men have realized that time has upset many fighting faiths, they may come to believe even more than they believe the very foundations of their own conduct that the ultimate good desired is better reached by free trade in ideas—that the best test of truth is the power of the thought to get itself accepted in the competition of the market, and that truth is the only ground upon which their wishes safely can be carried out."

But, after we have emerged from the spell of patriotic emotion caused by Justice Holmes' eloquent digression, it becomes necessary to remind ourselves again that the question before the Court was whether there was enough substantial evidence, even under Judge Holmes' rule, to justify the trial Judge in submitting the case to the jury on the question of intent.

The striking phraseology of that part of his opinion vindicating the wisdom of the doctrine of freedom of speech has diverted the attention of some of the most vigorous critics of the conclusion of the majority of the Court from the real question in the case. The chief among these critics, Professor Chafee, has devoted forty pages of a book on "Freedom of Speech," to a consideration of the question as to "how the *Abrams* trial and its outcome accord with a just administration of the criminal law." After a sweeping criticism of the attitude of the majority of the Court, he deplores the injustice to the defendants, but himself takes comfort, and then allays the fear which his criticism may have aroused in others, by the anti-climactic statement that the effect of the decision "on the legal conception of freedom of speech should be temporary in view of its meagre discussion of the subject and the enduring qualities of the reasoning of Justice Holmes." Why, then, we may ask, is it necessary to pour forth pages of irrelevant reasoning and denunciation whose principal tendency is to impair the confidence of the people in the highest Court of the land? If the trial Judge had in his discretion imposed a lighter sentence (with which the Supreme Court had nothing to do), and Justice Holmes had contented himself with discussing the question whether, under the rule he himself announced in the *Schenck, Frohwerk* and *Debs* cases, the facts in the *Abrams* case justified the submission of the case to the jury and had omitted his eloquent and inspiring, if irrelevant, discourse on the Freedom of Speech, the *Abrams* case would probably not have assumed, as it has in the minds of some critics, the epochal importance of the *Wilkes* case.

The next case decided by the Supreme Court was *Schaeffer* v. *United States*,[10] where the defendants were accused of wilfully falsifying telegraphic dispatches with the ultimate result and intent of hampering the United States in raising armies and conducting the War. Referring to the article on which the prosecution was based, Justice McKenna, delivering

[10]251 U. S. 466.

the opinion of the Court, said that "its statements were deliberate and wilfully false, the purpose being to represent that the War was not demanded by the people but was the result of the machinations of executive power, and thus to arouse resentment to it and what it would demand of ardor and effort." Justices Holmes, Brandeis and Clark dissented. Justice Brandeis wrote a dissenting opinion, in which Holmes, J., concurred. He refers to the "clear and present danger" test, and he concludes that the evidence did not justify the jury "acting in calmness" in finding "either that they [the acts] would obstruct, or that they would promote the success of the enemies of the United States." On the contrary, he thinks the jury "must have supposed it to be within their province to condemn men not merely for disloyal acts but for a disloyal heart; provided only that the disloyal heart was evidenced by some utterance. To prosecute men for such publications reminds of the days when men were hanged for constructive treason." And he concludes that "convictions such as these, besides abridging freedom of speech, threaten freedom of thought and of belief." But the position already alluded to of Justice Clark (who believed that the jury had not been correctly instructed) seems more consonant with the facts, that is, that the case involved no such serious consequences but was an ordinary case involving the question whether a jury could reasonably infer guilt.

The case of *Pierce* v. *The United States*,[11] decided in March, 1920, remains to be examined. The prosecution in this case grew out of the distribution in New York State by the defendants of a pamphlet called "The Price We Pay," which was prepared by a Socialist organization in Chicago. The pamphlet was a "highly colored and sensational document," picturing in lurid terms the horrors of war and in juxtaposition making such statements as this: "Conscription is upon us; the draft law is a fact. Into your homes the recruiting officers are coming. They will take your sons of military age and impress them into the army." And there are many statements of unquestioned fact, but coupled with dreadful rhetorical pictures, referring to a "seething swamp of torn flesh and floating entrails" into which the conscripted men will be plunged "screaming as they go." And then there is the conclusion: "And still the recruiting officers will come; seizing age after age, mounting up to the elder ones and taking the younger ones as they grow to soldier size. . . . The manhood of America gazes at that seething heaving swamp of bloody carrion in Europe, and says, 'Must we—be that.' . . . You cannot avoid it; you are being dragged, whipped, lashed, hurled into it."

These statements introduced the conclusion that the realization of the awful predictions of the pamphlet could be avoided by establishing Socialism; and the claim was made, as a similar claim was made in the *Abrams* case, that that and not the obstruction of the prosecution of the War was the primary purpose of the pamphlet. But it was also shown that with some of the pamphlets there was also distributed a circular issued by the Socialist party in which it is stated: "This organization has opposed war and conscription. It is still opposed to war and conscription. . . . Do you want to help in this struggle?"

---

[11]252 U. S. 239.

Justice Pitney, writing the opinion of the Court,[12] held that the defendants knowing the contents of the pamphlet were to have attributed to them an intent, and justified the conclusion that they attempted, "to bring about any and all such consequences as reasonably might be anticipated from its distribution," and that "whether the printed words would in fact produce as a proximate result a material interference with the recruiting or enlistment service, or the operation or success of the forces of the United States, was a question for the jury to decide in view of all the circumstances of the time and considering the place and manner of distribution." And in support of this conclusion the principle of the decision in the *Schenck, Frohwerk* and *Debs* cases was relied on.

To the argument so frequently made in Espionage cases that the defendants said nothing new but only repeated comments upon matters of public concern, the Court said:

"In effect it would allow the professed advocate of disloyalty to escape responsibility for statements, however audaciously false, so long as he did but reiterate what had been said before; while his ignorant dupes, believing his statements and thereby persuaded to obstruct the recruiting or enlistment service, would be punishable by fine or imprisonment under the same section."

Justice Brandeis, in writing the dissenting opinion[13] in which Justice

---

[12]"If its (the pamphlet's) probable effect was at all disputable, at least the jury fairly might believe that, under the circumstances existing, it would have a tendency to cause insubordination, disloyalty, and refusal of duty in the military and naval forces of the United States; that it amounted to an obstruction of the recruiting and enlistment service; and that it was intended to interfere with the success of our military and naval forces in the war in which the United States was then engaged. Evidently it was intended, as the jury found, to interfere with the conscription and recruitment services; to cause men eligible for the service to evade the draft; to bring home to them, and especially to their parents, sisters, wives, and sweethearts, a sense of impending personal loss, calculated to discourage the young men from entering the service; to arouse suspicion as to whether the chief law officer of the Government was not more concerned in enforcing the strictness of military discipline than in protecting the people against improper speculation in their food supply; and to produce a belief that our participation in the War was the product of sordid and sinister motives, rather than a design to protect the interests and maintain the honor of the United States."

[13]"A verdict should have been directed for the defendants on these counts also because the leaflet was not distributed under such circumstances, nor was it of such a nature as to create a clear and present danger of causing either insubordination, disloyalty, mutiny or refusal of duty in the military or naval forces. The leaflet contains lurid and perhaps exaggerated pictures of the horrors of war. Its arguments as to the causes of this war may appear to us shallow and grossly unfair. The remedy proposed may seem to us worse than the evil which, it is argued, will be thereby removed. But the leaflet, far from counselling disobedience to law, points to the hopelessness of protest, under the existing system, pictures the irresistible power of the military arm of the Government, and indicates that acquiescence is a necessity. Insubordination, disloyalty, mutiny and refusal of duty in the military or naval forces are very serious crimes. It is not conceivable that any man of ordinary intelligence and normal judgment would be induced by anything in the leaflet to commit them and thereby risk the severe punishment prescribed for such offenses. Certainly there was no clear and present danger that such would be the result. The leaflet was not even distributed among those in the military or the naval service. It was distributed among civilians; and since the conviction on the first count has been abandoned here by the Government, we have no occasion to consider whether the leaflet might have discouraged voluntary enlistment or obedience to the provisions of the Selective Draft Act."

Holmes concurred, rested his conclusions largely upon a strict application of the "clear and present danger" rule of the *Schenck* case. As to the charge of conspiracy he held that there was no evidence of evil intent except in the pamphlet itself and that was insufficient to justify its submission to the jury. He said it was "not conceivable that any man of ordinary intelligence and normal judgment would be induced by anything in the leaflet to commit them [i. e., crimes] and thereby risk the severe punishment prescribed for such offenses. Certainly there was no clear and present danger that such would be the result."

I do not go into the detail of Justice Brandeis' argument in support of his conclusions. It is only necessary to add that here, as in the *Schaeffer* case, the case presented a great variety of circumstances and the only question was whether they permitted divergent inferences which a jury should be permitted to pass upon.

I have now concluded my examination of the leading decisions of the Supreme Court under Article I, Sections 3 and 4 of the Espionage Act. Can it reasonably be said that they have tended to the disintegration of one of the foundation stones of our constitutional structure? An answer to this question requires a survey of the circumstances under which the Espionage Act was passed.

The World War was fought under conditions never before paralleled in history. The magnitude of military and naval operations required the conscription of all the potential economic and industrial resources of this country. It soon became, or at least seemed, manifest that even if the man power of the nation could have been recruited by voluntary enlistment, that method of creating an army could not successfully be adopted, and certainly not without impairing the efficiency of our industrial life. It was just as important to maintain production at home as it was to supply men for the front. Out of this situation grew the draft under the Selective Service Law, under which the civilian population coöperated in selecting a great army from their own numbers and in their own localities, and with a minimum of impairment of the efficiency of essential industries. Never before in the history of warfare was a draft so scientifically conceived and so successfully carried through. But it required the coöperation of the great mass of our citizenry. And obstruction, or even too freely expressed discouragement or disapproval, needed little to give it the aspect of interference with military preparations. As Justice Holmes said of the circulation of the paper in the *Frohwerk* case, it might have been "in quarters where a little breath would be enough to kindle a flame."

Before we entered the War we had learned what an important part propaganda was playing in the great struggle to preserve modern civilization. Germany especially had never ceased to rely upon it as one of the most potent weapons behind the lines of their enemies. And one of its most subtly dangerous features was a skillful camouflage by which the real purpose of disloyal literature was so cloaked as to make it appear, as was attempted in the *Abrams* and *Pierce* cases, to have an innocent purpose. Thus Germany openly announced that "bribery of enemies' subjects, acceptances of offers of treachery, utilization of discontented elements in the population, support of pretenders and the like, are permissible; indeed, international law is in no way opposed to the exploitation of the crimes of third parties." (German War Book—Morgan Translation, p. 85).

In this country there were millions of American citizens of German and Austrian birth or descent, and before we entered the War many of these had evinced their sympathy with the cause of the Central powers. While the great body of these citizens remained loyal and contributed their full share to the success of our arms, there were some who remained at heart in sympathy with Germany, some who were apathetic, and some who were undoubtedly disloyal in thought and only lacked the opportunity to be disloyal in act.

The Bolshevist propaganda was also constantly revealing itself and was resorted to as openly as personal safety would permit. Socialist opposition to the War was more open and candid than German propaganda. In the *Abrams* case it was sought to show that the writings had no direct relation to our war with Germany. But at the time it was necessary to conserve all our national resources. And any impairment of the efficiency of our essential industries by the introduction of Soviet principles or by general strikes, sabotage or other manifestations of discontent, could hardly avoid the effect of interfering with our war activities, and this was so obvious that an attribution of criminal intent required little additional evidence to support it. Such evidence was ample in the *Abrams* case.

Probably never before have so many causes combined to justify this country in adopting temporary repressive measures. The few provisions of the Sedition Laws of 1798 which survived and the statute defining treason had served in previous emergencies the purpose of national self-protection. But it soon became manifest that they were not adequate to prevent obstruction of the draft and the marshalling of our resources for the unprecedented struggle. Mr. O'Brian, the Special Assistant of the Attorney-General for war work, has said that we "had on our statute books almost no protection against hostile activities." It was a clear case for the application of the principle, long ago stated by Madison, that it is "vain to oppose constitutional barriers to the impulse of self-preservation." And few now seriously doubt that in 1917 measures of national self-preservation were necessary. No law of the kind was necessary in the Revolutionary War, the War of 1812, the Mexican War, the Civil War or the Spanish War, because the conditions in this country, and the methods of warfare on either side, did not require it. But the necessity for the Espionage Act was soon shown by the number of cases that it became necessary to prosecute.[14]

It has been charged that in some of the earlier cases under the Espionage Act, incorrect rules were applied by trial Judges; that Circuit Courts of Appeals did not hew to the correct line of judicial interpretation; that juries showed evidence of permitting patriotic emotion to influence their deliberations unduly, and that there was undue severity in imposing sentences. Justice Holmes showed that the length of the sentence in the *Abrams* case was not absent from his mind when he was formulating the most frequently quoted portion of his dissenting opinion; and the

[14]Nearly 2,000 cases were commenced in 1918 and 1919, and up to June 30, 1919, according to the report of the Attorney-General, there had been nearly 900 convictions.

sentence in that case certainly did not err on the side of excessive leniency. It may be the fact that in individual cases under the Espionage Act errors were made by trial Courts in instructing juries as to the nature and extent of the protection afforded by the First Amendment. But that should not be a source of discouragement to the lovers of liberty; for the subject was to a great extent new to American jurisprudence, as, happily for us, never before has an occasion arisen requiring our Courts to give so much attention to the subject. It is not strange if judges, though firm believers in the doctrine of freedom of speech in its historical and philosophical aspect, should not always succeed in correctly formulating its limitations when applied to concrete instances. But I venture to think that, if occasion should again arise, the discussions in the recent decisions of the Supreme Court under the Espionage Act are landmarks in our Constitutional jurisprudence which will be found to define in a practical way the division line which must separate the freedom of speech protected by the First Amendment and the licentiousness which may legally be prohibited by statute.

To enter upon an examination of the proceedings in the lower Courts would extend this address beyond its suitable limits. If errors have been committed, or if through local conditions, or by reason of prejudice or passion, exact justice has not always been meted out, that is because our judicial system is a human institution and, therefore, not perfect. But if in extending to persons charged with crime the protection of the Constitution the Supreme Court has stood staunch, we need not fear for the safety of our liberties.[15]

Some of the comments upon the results in the Espionage cases reveal a lack of confidence in our judicial system. I append some of these criticisms in a note.[16] I mention them only because they tend to con-

---

[15] John Lord O'Brian, Assistant Attorney-General, says: "In default of authoritative decisions by the Supreme Court, with eighty-eight Federal districts, each equipped with a United States Attorney and at least one District Judge, and the great variety of conditions peculiar to the respective localities, it is only strange that there did not develop greater divergencies in the character of prosecutions as well as the character of the decisions by the lower Courts. . . . A review of the rulings of the Courts on questions of evidence and a scrutiny of the charges to juries will show the future commentator that United States District Judges were keenly alive to this danger, (i. e., that there should not be 'fair and impartial trials'). They continually emphasized constitutional rights, gave great latitude to defendants' proof and urged necessity for the dispassionate consideration of evidence. . . . The ordinary procedure of our Courts functioned well. The efficacy of juries as triers of fact has been once more demonstrated in a convincing manner, and the highest praise is not too much for the Federal Judiciary who, with only a few exceptions, taking a broad view of the necessities of the country, still maintained the American tradition of fairness and went to extremes in enforcing consideration of the constitutional guarantees." (Address before the New York State Bar Association, Vol. 42, of the Annual Reports).

[16] Thus it is said that in time of war the protection of a jury trial is illusory. Professor Chafee is disturbed because Judge Clayton, a Judge of character and ability with a distinguished public career, was assigned to try the *Abrams* case, although it was his first prominent case of the kind, while there were three other District Court Judges who had had "extensive experience in the difficulties of War legislation." Furthermore, he thought the position of the defendants "could hardly be understood without some acquaintance with the immigrant population of a great city, some knowledge of the ardent thirst of the East Side Jew for the discussion of international affairs. Yet because the New York dockets were crowded the

15

firm what I have already said, that is that, after all, the questions arising under the Espionage Act largely involve ordinary matters of judicial procedure, not vital questions of civil liberty. And the differences between the Justices of the Supreme Court, when analyzed, will be found to relate not to great questions of constitutional law, but to differing ideas as to deductions from proven facts.

Words that we regard as impious, disloyal, revolutionary or obscene, produce in most of us a natural, if temporary, reaction, in which the remedy of repression first suggests itself. We do not readily rely upon the unwisdom of applying the law of seditious libel under a form of government like ours. We do not recall the warning of the *Wilkes* case, or the history of the constitutional struggles in England, by which freedom of speech became the heritage of our ancestors. Neither do the ancient lessons taught by the death of Socrates, or the unanswerable logic of Mill and Milton on freedom of opinion, occur to us. The natural impulse is to adopt the simplest and quickest method of repression. Many intelligent persons who would indignantly deny that they would change the guaranties of our Bill of Rights are among the first to denounce seditious utterauces and to favor laws to prevent them. This human tendency has led to persecutions of all kinds in the past.

But after centuries of experience we have worked out a practical solution of the vexed question, and we now believe that, both as a matter of inherent individual right and of political and social expediency, opinion and its free expression should not be restrained except so far as that may be necessary for the preservation of order and the protection of the State. Experience shows that error, if repressed, gains factitious strength. The repression confirms it in those who are forced to be silent, while those who could dispel it lack the opportunity. Justice Holmes has used a striking figure on the subject when he said

"With effervescing opinions, as with the not yet forgotten champagnes, the quickest way to let them get flat is to let them get exposed to the air."

We see in our political life repeated instances of the power of discussion to dispel error. To mention only one, we all remember the proposed recall of judges and decisions which was pressed with extraordinary earnestness and persistence. It was a fallacy affecting the proper function of the judiciary in our system which presented great danger to our institutions. The discussion which it excited resulted in the complete exposure to all of the fallacy on which it was founded; and its advo-

Abrams case was assigned to a judge who had tried no important Espionage Act case, who was called in from a remote district where people were of one mind about the War, where the working class is more conspicuous for a submissive respect for law and order than for the criticism of high officials, where Russians are scarce and Bolshevists unknown." This same critic continues that if we are going to continue to "prosecute men for the bad political tendency of their disloyal or anarchistic utterances," that is, under the rule of procedure approved by the Supreme Court, it may be advisable to adopt the "wide open policy" of evidence in use in France, where parties and witnesses express "fully and unhindered." This comment was made with reference to the exclusion of testimony, which Professor Chafee admits was proper "in the absence of any established technique for political crimes in this country," but that made it necessary for the Judge to have "pounded home" the proposition that the subject excluded had nothing to do with the case.

cates were themselves persuaded of their error. If the agitation had been met with smug complacency, or by repression, it might have prevailed, or remained unsettled as a future menace. Discontent with our Courts will undoubtedly again arise in some other form—indeed, it has already arisen, as I have shown, on their treatment of the subject of free speech. The best way to meet it is to discuss it, to make opinion liquid as water, free as air, and not by repression to freeze opinion into prejudice.

But my chief theme to-day is free speech in War time, especially bearing upon political rights in a representative democracy. The safety of such a State as ours rests in unrestrained discussion of any subject affecting it. But neither the State nor any public officer is sacrosanct, as they are in a monarchy where the permanency of the State depends in part on the sacred character of the sovereign, and free criticism easily becomes sedition. Yet in this country seditious libel has practically departed from our jurisprudence. And the most valuable field for free speech is unrestrained discussion of public affairs and public men; and so long as there is no violation of the law of libel, such discussion is without restriction. If this results in unfairness, in misrepresentation, in intemperate abuse, in glaring breaches of good taste and in other partisan excesses which our political contests evoke, we must depend upon time and discussion, working on the minds of the people finally aroused to exercise independent judgment, to allay animosities, to soften asperities, to condemn the intemperate, to discover the fundamental element of truth and finally to come to an approximately correct conclusion.

With the complexities of our modern civilization increasing obstacles are placed in the way of the free play of public opinion. For illustration I mention one of the obstacles I refer to. Mr. Cobb, the Editor of the New York World, in December, 1919, said that there were 1,200 private press agents engaged in business in New York, and he asserts that "many direct channels to news have been closed and the information for the public is first filtered through publicity agents. The great corporations have them, the banks have them, the railroads have them, all the organizations of business and of social and political activity have them, and they are the media through which news comes. Even statesmen have them." And so in times of peace we must exercise patience, and try to believe that in the long run substantial error will be detected and truth and sanity will prevail. But during the late War patience was not always possible. The emergency did not permit delay. We could not depend upon time and free discussion to eliminate error and vindicate truth. We were engaged in the greatest struggle of our history. We believed, rightly or wrongly, that our institutions and our liberties—yes, modern civilization—were at stake. We had to have a gigantic army; we couldn't wait. We had to get it through the instrumentality of our present form of government; we couldn't stop to examine the advantages of the Soviet plan, and, as a practical matter, mere discussion of that subject tended to impair the efficiency of our essential industries and, therefore, our fighting strength. It was too late to discuss the merits of the War. The die was cast. We had to fight, not discuss. And everyone realized that under the circumstances it would take little to "fan the flame" and produce indifference, inefficiency or disloyalty.

Under such circumstances it would have been absurd to stop to hunt out the ignorant foreigners among whom *Abrams* distributed his inflammatory circular and persuade each of them by reason that it was based on an economic fallacy; or to correct maliciously falsified dispatches calculated to discourage our War operations; or to remove the impression of Pierce's dreadful circulars upon registrants. It became necessary, as one of the despairing critics has said, for the government to conscript public opinion, as it conscripted men and material. But conscription in any sense of the word is no longer necessary. The technical continuance of a state of war affords little reason for retaining laws to prevent obstruction of the operations of our military forces or of our recruiting service. The retention of such laws may give comfort to some, and in the present situation they are perhaps innocuous, unless, indeed, it is supposed that they may be useful in combating Communistic movements against our government. But, while it is true that Russian Bolshevism asserts that it cannot continue unless all the world is made Communistic, and, if necessary, by force, no hostile invasion is possible except by propaganda. Now that the War is over, however, and such propaganda cannot weaken our military resources, I believe that Communism can best be fought by argument, and not by repression. It stands for a destruction of the sanctity of private contracts and of the principle of private property; it conscripts labor so as to create a veritable condition of slavery; and it abolishes the right of inheritance. It suppresses in the individual all desire through initiative and thrift to improve his physical, mental or moral condition. If such doctrines as these are subjected to the test of free discussion they cannot flourish in this country. What is needed is a dissemination of its literature showing the real nature of Bolshevism, and a frank discussion which will enlighten the masses of our people as to its real meaning. There may be discontent and occasional disorder, but if the American people will seriously concern themselves to combat such heresies, they not only will wither away, but we will have a most healthful exhibition of the power of unrestrained discussion.

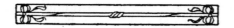